THE SCIENCE OF A SPIRAL

NEL YOMTOV

Published in the United States of America by Cherry Lake Publishing
Ann Arbor, Michigan
www.cherrylakepublishing.com

Content Adviser: Erik Zobel, Amherst High School Physics, Amherst, New York
Reading Adviser: Marla Conn, ReadAbility, Inc.

Photo Credits: © Air Images/Shutterstock Images, cover, 1; © Yobro10 | Dreamstime.com, 5; © Aspenphoto | Dreamstime.com, 6; © Michael Langish/Shutterstock.com, 9; © Matt Howard/Shutterstock Images, 10; © eyecrave/ iStock Images, 13; © Jaboardm | Dreamstime.com - Quarterback Pass Football Photo, 14; © Aspen Photo/Shutterstock Images, 16; © Michael Dinovo/Cal Sport Media/ZUMA Press/Newscom, 19; © Richard Paul Kane/Shutterstock.com, 20; © Jeremy R. Smith Sr./Shutterstock.com, 22; © Swa1959 | Dreamstime.com - Brett Favre Photo, 25; © Goldnelk | Dreamstime.com - Peyton Manning Passes Photo, 26; © American Spirit/Shutterstock.com, 28

Library of Congress Cataloging-in-Publication Data

Yomtov, Nelson.
  The science of a spiral/Nel Yomtov.
    pages cm.—(Full-Speed Sports)
  Includes index.
  ISBN 978-1-63362-585-3 (hardcover)—ISBN 978-1-63362-765-9 (pdf)—ISBN 978-1-63362-675-1 (paperback)—
ISBN 978-1-63362-855-7 (ebook)
  1. Passing (Football)—Juvenile literature. I. Title.

  GV951.5.Y66 2015
  796.332'25—dc23
                            2014048651

Cherry Lake Publishing would like to acknowledge the work of
the Partnership for 21st Century Skills. Please visit www.p21.org
for more information.

Printed in the United States of America
Corporate Graphics

ABOUT THE AUTHOR

Nel Yomtov is an award-winning author of nonfiction books and graphic novels for young readers. He lives in the New York City area.

TABLE OF CONTENTS

CHAPTER 1

THE LONG BOMB

Dale was excited to be at his first professional football game with his father. They were watching their favorite team, the Minnesota Vikings. The Vikings were behind by a score of 24–21 with only 15 seconds to play, but they had the ball—and a chance to win.

"We have to go 80 yards for a touchdown," Dale said, worried. "Do you think we can do it?"

"Maybe, but it would take a **bomb**, a long pass," his dad replied. "Look, the last play is starting!"

As everyone in the stadium rose to their feet, a tense quiet settled over the huge crowd. The Vikings' **quarterback** shouted signals, took the **snap** from the center, and dropped back to pass. The defense charged, but the quarterback stayed calm and looked downfield for an open receiver.

The last couple minutes of a game are sometimes the most exciting.

A successful quarterback needs good receivers to catch his passes.

"Throw the ball! Throw the ball!" Dale shouted.

The clock ticked down: 10 seconds, 9, 8, 7 . . .

Suddenly, the quarterback stepped forward and launched a long pass to a receiver speeding along the sideline. Amazingly, the perfectly thrown ball settled into his outstretched hands—60 yards (55 meters) away! The receiver raced toward the goal line, hotly pursued by two defenders.

"TOUCHDOWN!" Dale screamed. "A perfect pass! We won, Dad, we won!"

Of the many different skills required of football players, throwing the ball, or passing, might be the most difficult to master. The goal of the passer, the quarterback, is to throw the ball as accurately as possible, usually with high speed and over long distances. It sounds simple, but how does he do it?

He does it by throwing a **spiral**. That's the name for a perfectly thrown, rapidly spinning pass that moves smoothly, seemingly without effort, through the air. To make this so-called perfect pass, a quarterback must understand and master the physical forces involved in throwing a football.

And it all starts with the ball itself.

GO DEEPER!

Read the paragraph about a spiral again. What is the main idea? What is one of the most difficult skills for a football player to acquire? When passing, what is a quarterback's goal? Are there physical forces that are involved in throwing a football? If so, can you tell what they are by reading the paragraph?

CHAPTER 2

An Oddly Shaped Ball

Compare the balls used in most sports today. They have one thing in common: their shape. The balls used in baseball, tennis, soccer, basketball, volleyball, lacrosse, and bowling are **spherical**. Why is a football such a peculiar shape? You can blame it on a pig.

The first organized game of football took place on November 6, 1869, between Rutgers and Princeton Universities in New Jersey. The rules were based on the sport of rugby, where they players kick the ball, so early footballs reflected that: round, with a slightly

Modern-day footballs have pointy ends and white laces.

oval shape. These footballs were made from inflated pig bladders, which is why footballs are sometimes called pigskins.

Later, the inflated bladders were covered in leather made from cowhide. The leather made the ball more **durable**, so it could withstand the stress of a game. Laces held the leather skin together. Today, the lacing doesn't hold the ball together, but it allows the players to better grip the ball and throw it farther and more accurately.

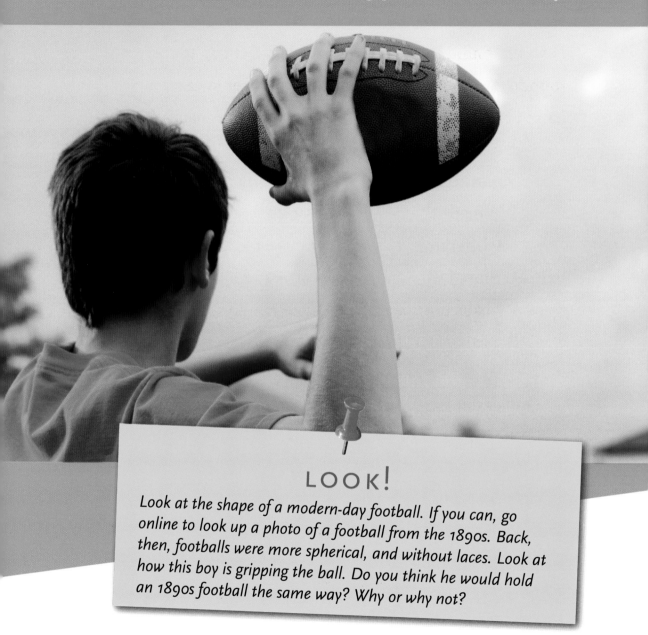

The white lacing helps the quarterback grip the ball to throw it correctly.

LOOK!

Look at the shape of a modern-day football. If you can, go online to look up a photo of a football from the 1890s. Back, then, footballs were more spherical, and without laces. Look at how this boy is gripping the ball. Do you think he would hold an 1890s football the same way? Why or why not?

In the late 19th century, American football began to focus on carrying the ball, rather than kicking it. Players, however, found it **awkward** and often difficult to carry a roundish, rugby-style ball. To make it easier to carry a ball in the bend of the arm, balls began to be made in a slightly **elongated** shape, like an egg.

The **evolution** of the football marched on. In 1906, new rules made the forward pass a legal play. Players needed a differently shaped ball that allowed a better grip but also moved through the air easily and quickly. Over time, footballs evolved into the more pointed, or oblong, football used today. Mathematicians call the shape of a modern football a prolate spheroid.

The reason for making the ball more pointed was to make it easier to throw and more **aerodynamic**. Yet the ball's oblong shape also makes the ball very **unstable** in the air. To stabilize the ball, the spiral is needed: the special spin that balances the forces of nature and allows the ball to travel through the air more easily.

CHAPTER 3

THE SCIENCE OF THE SPIRAL

A quarterback throwing a football—or anyone throwing anything in the air—must deal with two natural forces: gravity and air resistance, or **drag**. Gravity is the force that pulls the ball toward the earth. It's the same force that keeps your feet on the ground, your laptop in your lap, and your dinner plate on the kitchen table.

Air resistance is the force of air against a moving object. The air around us is made of molecules and atoms. When an object moves, it pushes against the molecules and atoms in the air. The molecules do not

The pointy tips of a football, along with the spin given when it's thrown, help it fly smoothly through the air.

move aside quickly. Instead, they slow down the object. The force that resists the motion of an object is called drag, or air resistance.

The oblong shape of the football, however, provides it with a reduced frontal surface. The smaller surface at the ball's tip means fewer air molecules push against the ball as it travels forward. This means less drag and easier movement through the air.

But how do you keep a football stabilized and pointing in the right direction? That's where spin comes in.

A quarterback can have a tough time throwing a good spiral when his opponents are trying to tackle him.

Dr. William J. Rae, a professor at the State University of New York at Buffalo, has studied the flight movements of the football. Rae observed that a properly thrown football spins on its axis—an imaginary line that runs lengthwise through the two tips of the ball. A well-thrown ball can spin 400 to 600 times a minute around its axis.

Once the ball is in flight, it begins a complex interaction with the forces of nature. Rae analyzed super-slow-motion videotapes of forward passes.

He discovered that as the ball spins, gravity and the movement of air around the ball cause it to first move slightly to the right, then down a little, then to the left, then up a little, and then to the right again. It's a spiral, but there's a hint of wobble. As the front of the football rotates, the ball is stabilized and kept on track. This unique action is called **gyroscopic torque**, or the tendency of a force or forces to keep an object rotating on its axis.

That's the science of a spiral, but what's the best way to throw one?

THINK ABOUT IT!

The wind direction can play a huge role in the quarterback's ability to throw the ball. If the wind is blowing opposite the direction the quarterback throws the ball, that creates drag. What do you think happens if the wind blows in the same direction the ball is moving? What if the wind comes from the side? Can you think of ideal conditions for a quarterback to throw the ball the furthest?

To make a good pass, the quarterback must keep his eye on the target.

First, take a relaxed grip of the ball, so that your ring finger and little finger are across the laces and the thumb is underneath. Hold the ball with the fingertips, not the palm. Point your front shoulder at your target, and turn your hips to the side you throw with.

As you step forward, open your hips to the side. Let your arm come forward and release the ball, rolling it out with your fingertips while snapping the wrist. Rotate your thumb toward the opposite thigh. Make sure to follow through, with your index finger being the last thing off of the ball. After the release, the thumb should be pointing down, indicating you had rotated the ball counterclockwise. Practice makes perfect—you'll get better with each new throw.

CHAPTER 4

PLAYING IT SAFE

In an average National Football League game, a quarterback might throw 30 or 40 passes, sometimes more. During practices leading up to game day, he will throw dozens more than that. Over many seasons, it adds up to hundreds of thousands of throws. That's a lot of wear and tear on the quarterback's shoulder.

According to Dr. B. Wayne McGough Jr., a surgeon at the Andrews Sports Medicine and Orthopaedic Center in Birmingham, Alabama, throwing a football is less harmful to the shoulder than throwing a baseball.

"The throwing motion of a football requires less extreme ranges of motion. When you're not pushing your shoulder to extreme ranges of external rotation or internal rotation, it's less likely to lead to injury," said McGough.

A quarterback who injures his shoulder can take a long time to recover.

A quarterback who often gets sacked has a high chance of getting injured.

[21ST CENTURY SKILLS LIBRARY]

That's the good news. But in the violent world of professional football, quarterbacks risk colliding with an opponent or being slammed to the ground by 300-pound (136 kilograms) defensive linemen. "About 80 percent of shoulder injuries are due to direct **trauma**," like **sacks**, added McGough.

Although shoulder injuries due to overuse are not as common in football as they are in baseball, there is still cause for concern. This is especially true of the young athlete, whose muscles, tendons, and ligaments have not reached peak strength. Constant, repetitive

GO DEEPER!

Think about what you've just read. Is throwing a football more harmful to the shoulder than throwing a baseball? Do you think the quarterback position is a dangerous one? Why? What is the cause of most quarterback shoulder injuries? How important is proper form to avoiding injury? Name a few strategies quarterbacks use to avoid shoulder injury.

Players should learn safe throwing techniques when they're young.

[21ST CENTURY SKILLS LIBRARY]

stress on the shoulder, such as throwing, may tear or overstretch these structures or damage joints.

Poor form in the throwing motion can also lead to injuries. To avoid injury, most NFL quarterbacks make sure the elbow is at ear height when they release the ball. The arm should be fully extended after the release, not before. The elbow should never be higher than the ball at any time, even when just bringing back the arm to throw. Finally, the forward stride when releasing the ball should not be too long. A long stride causes the release to be too far in front of the body. That creates stress in the shoulder.

Experts agree that a reasonable number of throws performed with proper form are not a problem. However, even a few throws with incorrect form can cause damage.

CHAPTER 5

MASTER PASSERS

Completing a long pass—the bomb—is football's version of a grand slam in baseball or a breakaway goal in hockey. In one super-exciting, all-or-nothing moment, it can mean the difference between defeat and victory. The quarterback must launch a near-perfect spiral, often with speedy, fearsome defenders closing in fast. The pass must reach a spot far downfield— to a point where the receiver will not even arrive for several more seconds.

Brett Favre, of the Green Bay Packers, is one of the game's most outstanding quarterbacks.

Completing nearly any type of forward pass requires skill, timing, good judgment, and coordination. Over the decades, many great quarterbacks have played in the NFL. But who are the best of the best?

Brett Favre, Peyton Manning, and Dan Marino all have impressive statistics. In a career spanning from 1991 to 2010, Favre is the all-time leader in pass completions (6,300) and passing yards with 71,838— that's nearly 50 miles (80.5 km)! Manning's career began in 1998 with the Indianapolis Colts. He later played for

Peyton Manning is known for his strong passing abilities.

the Denver Broncos. Manning is the NFL's all-time leader in touchdown passes (530 at the end of the 2014 season). Marino, who played his entire career with the Miami Dolphins, from 1983 to 1999, ranks third all-time in touchdowns passes, passing yards, and passes completed.

The number of championships is another way to judge quarterbacks' skills. Terry Bradshaw, Joe Montana, Troy Aikman, and Tom Brady have all led their teams to multiple championship wins. Playing for the Pittsburgh Steelers from 1970 to 1983, Bradshaw won an incredible four Super Bowls—without a loss—in a six-year period. Montana matched Bradshaw, leading the San Francisco 49ers to four Super Bowl championships, also without a loss. Aikman had a 3–0 record in Super Bowl games, leading the Dallas Cowboys to titles in 1993, 1994, and 1996. In more recent years, Tom Brady has taken the New England Patriots to six Super Bowl games, winning four (including the 2015 game) while losing two.

THINK ABOUT IT!

Sports are a major force in the lives of many people. Sports offer entertainment and health benefits, teach teamwork and fair play, and provide the opportunity to compete with others. Winning is part of sports, as the quarterbacks in this chapter would probably agree. But do you think there is an overemphasis on winning in our society? Does the pressure to win decrease the fun of playing sports?

Football has been a popular spectator sport for many years.

Many experts rank Drew Brees of the New Orleans
Saints as one of today's top quarterbacks. Brees is the only
quarterback in NFL history to throw for 5,000 yards in a
season more than once—he's done it four times! In 2010,
Brees led the Saints to their first-ever Super Bowl title.

One of the most awesome sights in the game of football
is the perfectly thrown spiral pass. There's nothing more
exciting than watching a quarterback launch a long, arcing
bomb downfield into the outstretched arms of a quick
receiver. It's truly a great moment for spectators and
players—and a remarkable example of science at work.

TIMELINE

A TIMELINE HISTORY OF FOOTBALL

1869	Rutgers University plays Princeton University in the first game of intercollegiate football. A roundish ball is used, and the rules of the game are similar to rugby.
Early 20th century	The first professional football leagues are established.
1906	The forward pass becomes legal. It has limited effectiveness because of the round shape of the ball.
1930s	The football becomes longer and slimmer.
1939	The National Football League (NFL) first uses plastic helmets.
1941	The official ball used by the NFL is nicknamed "The Duke," after New York Giants owner Wellington Mara, who was named after England's Duke of Wellington.
1956	The white balls traditionally used in night games are replaced with the standard daytime football circled by two white stripes.
1958	The Baltimore Colts and New York Giants play "The Greatest Game Ever Played"–the NFL's first-ever sudden death overtime. Over 50 million people watch it on TV.
2015	The New England Patriots are accused of using under-inflated footballs in the AFC Championship Game against the Indianapolis Colts. The media calls it "Deflategate."

THINK ABOUT IT

How has the shape of a football changed over the years? What were early footballs made of?

Read chapter 3 again. What are two natural forces a quarterback must deal with when making a pass? Describe the pattern that the nose of a football makes as it spins through the air.

Watch a football game on television and carefully study what the quarterback does. Describe the sequence of movements he makes from the time he receives the snap to the follow-through after releasing the ball.

LEARN MORE

LEARN MORE

Barr, George. *Sports Science for Young People*. New York: Dover Publications, 2011.

Biskup, Agnieszka. *Football: How It Works*. Mankato, MN: Capstone Press, 2010.

Hantula, Richard. *Science at Work in Football*. New York: Marshall Cavendish Benchmark, 2012.

WEB SITES

Exploratorium: Sport! Science
www.exploratorium.edu/sports/ask_us_sports_july.html
Learn why a football and a rugby ball travel differently through the air.

NFL Rush
http://www.nflrush.com/
Play games, read interviews, watch videos, and catch the latest fantasy football news on this just-for-kids sports site.

Science Kids—Sports Videos: The Perfect Spiral
www.sciencekids.co.nz/videos/sports/perfectspiral.html
Learn how to throw a perfect spiral pass from NFL superstar quarterback Drew Brees.

GLOSSARY

aerodynamic (air-oh-dye-NAM-ik) designed to move through the air very easily and quickly

awkward (AWK-wurd) difficult; not graceful or smooth

bomb (BAHM) in football, a very long pass

drag (DRAG) a force which slows down the movement of an object

durable (DOOR-uh-buhl) tough and lasting for a long time

elongated (i-LAWNG-gate-id) made longer or more stretched out

evolution (ev-uh-LOO-shuhn) gradual change or development into another form

gyroscopic torque (JYE-ruh-SKAH-pic TORK) the tendency of a force or forces to keep an object rotating on its axis

quarterback (KWOR-tur-bak) in football, the player who leads the offense by throwing the ball or handing it to a runner

sacks (SAKS) in football, moments when a quarterback is tackled by the opposing team before being able to throw a forward pass

snap (SNAP) in football, the action that begins a play in which the ball is handed to the quarterback

spherical (SFEER-i-kuhl) shaped like a globe

spiral (SPYE-ruhl) in football, a pass in which the ball spins around an imaginary axis running from tip to tip

trauma (TRAW-muh) a severe physical wound or injury

unstable (uhn-STAY-buhl) unsteady or shaky

INDEX